Conquering

Procrastination

How To Stay Motivated, Become More Productive And Cure Laziness Forever

By

Patrick Magana

Table of Contents

Introduction 5

Chapter 1 Procrastination 7

Executive Functions – Aka – Cognitive Control ...10

All Three Executive Functions Work Together 12

Chapter 2 Behavior Self-Regulation.... 21

Assessor And Locomotive Characteristics............ 22

Regulatory Behavior Characteristics Of
Procrastinators 26

**Chapter 3 How Thinking Contributes To
Procrastination................................. 34**

Perfectionism Can Lead To Burnout 38

**Chapter 4 Personality And
Procrastination – Is It Genetics? 43**

Twin Studies 44

The Role Of COMT In Procrastination................... 47

Does Serotonin Play A Role In Procrastination? . 50

Chapter 5 Changing Your Brain 54

Your Changing Brain 54

Getting Started Creates The Right Mood!............57

Costs And Consequences 59

Chapter 6 Improving (Slowly) 65

"Slow And Steady Wins The Race." 68

The Compound Effect – How The Little Things Add

Up 76

How Building Momentum Helps 83

Chapter 7 The Right Habits.................92

The Power In Taking Responsibility For Your

Actions 92

To Manage Something, You Must First Measure It

....94

Put Success On Autopilot By Establishing Good

Habits – The Can Approach 95

How To Build The Right Habits 101

How To Embrace A Routine Of Healthy Habits ..115

Chapter 8 Staying Motivated 123

Be Careful Who You Hang Out With....................123

How To Get And Stay Motivated..........................126

Types Of Internalization......................................133

Ways To Stay Motivated 138

Conclusion 144

References 148

Disclaimer 156

Introduction

Procrastination. That is why you are here, isn't it? By the time you have finished this book, you will have learned multiple new strategies for beating procrastination.

By employing simple techniques, you will soon find yourself able to tackle even the most overwhelming projects. You will learn how to turn the human brains psychological quirks into advantages. You will be able to use easy tricks for pacing yourself, developing and keeping motivation, and ultimately succeeding in your goals.

I have struggled with procrastination for many years. Throughout that time, I have done tons of research and have included some of the better papers to address procrastination. As a result, this book is backed up by decades of scientific research. I just need to share this information with you.

You will find a detailed overview of the causes and solutions to procrastination, from the biological and psychological origins to behavioral modifications.

Again, all backed up by science!

Your future will be forever changed because you will now understand the hows and whys behind procrastination.

Why are you waiting? The sooner you learn these techniques, the closer you will be to turning your life around!

Each chapter unlocks new information that you probably have never seen before. Utilizing it will improve your mood and outlook on life. You will be able to get more things done than you ever believed possible!

Chapter 1 Procrastination

Procrastination. You are probably procrastinating right now. Maybe you got bored with your latest essay assignment. Perhaps you became sick of analyzing data you need to for work. Or you could be putting off starting chores that you desperately need to finish.

Or maybe you saw this book out of the corner of your eye and thought "this book could help me!" At any rate, you are explaining away your decision to step away from other more important duties and are here reading this book now.

Everyone procrastinates. It seems to be an integral part of human nature. In fact, over 20 percent of adults in the United States are affected by chronic procrastination [30]. Even if you are not a chronic procrastinator, you could still be affected by situational procrastination. Either way, people do not want to be identified as a procrastinator. Most of us hate that we do it. But what *is* the technical definition of procrastination?

Merriam-Webster.com defines procrastination as 1) to put off intentionally and habitually, or, 2) to put off intentionally the doing of something that should be done [25]. So, procrastination occurs when you put something off on purpose and make a habit out of it; procrastination is when you purposely put off doing something that you need to do. The first definition describes a chronic procrastinator, while the second describes someone who procrastinates on occasion. Is there a more personal definition though?

Psychologytoday.com defines procrastinators as people who "chronically avoid difficult tasks and deliberately look for distractions."[26]. The more personal take is that procrastinators want to avoid hard tasks and they use distractions to prevent themselves from doing them. There are many reasons a procrastinator may not want to do a job: boredom, resentment, and burnout are a few of them.

Psychologytoday.com goes onto define three types of procrastinators: 1) arousal types (those who get a "rush" by waiting until the last minute to do something), 2) Avoiders (those who avoid tasks because they are scared of failure or what success may bring), and 3) decisional procrastinators (those who are not able to make a decision) [26]. Just as there is a wide variety of personalities, there are a variety of procrastinators. But what do they all have in common?

Researchers Tom Tibbett and Joseph Ferrari have the answer to that question. They say procrastination "is a common, sub-optimal decision-making strategy that emphasizes short-term benefits at the expense of later performance." [30]. In other words, people who procrastinate make poor decisions; they make decisions that make them feel good or help them now, but later on down the road, those actions will hurt them. People procrastinate because they want to finish a more straightforward task so they can see the results now.

Doing an easier task first will cause issues later. When you next start the critical job, you will have less energy and time to dedicate to it. As a result, the more crucial task will suffer in quality.

Why do people procrastinate when they know they shouldn't? In order to answer that, we need to cover the whys and hows of our behavior in brief.

Executive Functions – Aka – Cognitive Control

Executive functions (EFs) are the mental processes that you need to regulate your thoughts, your behaviors, and to concentrate on what you are doing [6]. The frontal lobe of the brain controls and monitors your behavior, attention, cognition (thoughts), and emotions [3] [5] [23]. EFs occur in the frontal lobe.

EFs can also be described as the ability to carry out tasks and process information that is related to obtaining your goals [22]. The actions you take and the thoughts that you have are considered to be EFs. You perform executive functions every day. From deciding what clothes to wear, what to say (and not say) to your boss and others around you, to what you think about the events occurring around you.

However, it is difficult to carry out executive functions as there is so much to pay attention to in your world. Going on "autopilot" and foregoing the mental effort is much easier to do [6]. If you go on autopilot though, then you will not be able to change your habits. You will not be able to ignore distractions. To live a successful life, you need to know how your executive functions work, and how to use them to improve your life.

There are three main types of executive functions: inhibition, working memory, and cognitive flexibility [23]. These base executive functions form the foundation for other higher order executive functions (reasoning, planning, and problem-solving) that you need to navigate throughout your day [6]. If there are cracks in our foundation (base EFs), then there will be cracks in our structures (higher level EFs).

Here, we will only focus on the base level EFs: inhibition, working memory, and cognitive flexibility.

All Three Executive Functions Work Together

In 2000, Miyake and colleagues set out and to investigate three suggested executive functions[23]. They succeeded in verifying them. They also discovered that each of these EFs are correlated with one another, but are still distinct [23]. In other words, all three can work together and separately simultaneously.

Inhibition

How is inhibition going to help? Weren't we trying to

get things done, not prevent us from doing them?

Well, inhibition allows you to regulate your attention, behavior, thoughts, and emotions in a controlled way; this enables you to complete necessary tasks [6] [23]. The different kinds of EF inhibition are inhibitory control, self-control (behavioral inhibition), selective attention interference control, and cognitive inhibition interference control [6].

All of this inhibitory control may seem like too much at first, but remember you are constantly bombarded with stimuli every day. If you did not filter anything out, you would be too overwhelmed to finish anything!

It feels like there are thousands, if not millions of distractions coming our way all of the time. Family. School. Work. Kids. Pets. Social Media. The Internet. Games. Phones. Your thoughts. Luckily, inhibition can help filter out this onslaught of information.

Inhibition – Inhibitory Control

Inhibitory control is the ability you have to steer your attention, behavior, thoughts, and emotions away from your internal and external desires [6]. This control allows you to do the most critical tasks first [6]. Inhibitory control is needed if you want to change your unhealthy habits, old ways of thinking, and avoid procrastinating. Without inhibitory control, you would not be able to assign priority to the tasks you need to do each day.

For instance, say you had a lot of essential errands to run: a critical letter that you *need* to mail today, renewing your driver's license, and an account needs to be closed today before the bank starts charging fees to keep it open. All of these are very dull, time-consuming tasks, but you need to do them all today.

But today is also the day that that new video game you have been waiting for is going to be released. All you want to do is buy it, and come home and tune out the

14

world so you can escape for a little while. Here, your internal desires are fighting with what you know you need to get done today. Inhibitory control allows you to push those desires aside so that those errands can get done and your life can go on.

Inhibition – Self Control (Behavior Inhibition)

Self-control, or behavior inhibition, is the control that you have over your behaviors and emotions [6]. If your boss is berating you time and time again, you may have the urge to one day to scream in his face and quit. Through behavior inhibition, you can squash those thoughts and keep your job.

Or, say you are growing bored with writing up a report for work, and you want to check Reddit. Being able to continue writing that report in spite of that temptation is how you can maintain self-control [6]. After all, you can always check out Reddit *after* you finish your work.

Inhibition – Selective Attention Interference Control

Paying attention to your surrounds is always essential. However, there is a possibility that you could pay attention to too many things. Selective attention interference control allows us to focus on one thing we want to when we are constantly barraged with various inputs [6]. This selective attention enables you to complete your work without being distracted by every noise you hear.

Think back to when you were a student (or maybe you still are one!). Your teacher may have just assigned you a group assignment and now wants everyone to discuss it in their respective groups. The entire class is now talking, and it is hard to single out individual voices. When you start to focus in on your group, the noise of the rest of the classroom falls to the wayside. This is selective attention.

Inhibition – Cognitive Inhibition Interference Control

And lastly, we have cognitive inhibition. Do you know those intrusive thoughts that pop up in your head that you can't get rid of? Those embarrassing memories you want to forget? Those self-doubts you have? You can control all of those by way of cognitive inhibition. Cognitive inhibition allows you to push those thoughts away so you can move on with your day [6].

Working Memory

Working memory (WM) allows you to process, update, and analyze information that relates to the current task you are performing[6] [10] [23]. After taking in new information, your working memory allows you to "delete" old data that is no longer relevant or needed [10] [23].

WM is used when you need to understand written or spoken language, do mental math, make lists, process plans, and, most importantly, when you need to reason and see connections between ideas and concepts [6]. Without WM, you would not be able to live a full and productive life.

Working Memory And Inhibitory Control

The executive functions working memory and inhibitory control also function in tandem [6] [23]. WM aids inhibitory control through goal management. If you want to know what thoughts you need to suppress, then you need to know what your current goals are [6].

Inhibitory control can prevent old information from working its way into WM; this allows your WM to focus only on current and topical facts [6]. Also, inhibitory control can "mute" or silence distractions so that your WM can more easily flow [6].

Say you are out shopping and you have a mental list of all the things you need to buy for the week's dinners.

You have prepared for multiple chicken dishes, but when you arrive at the store, you find that they have run out of chicken. Now you have to buy either beef or fish. You do not know any recipes for those meats, off the top of your head, that have the same main ingredients as those for chicken.

Inhibitory control now kicks in and prevents you from thinking of all of the chicken dish ingredients you were going to buy (even though you were looking forward to chicken!). Your working memory is now free to update the list in your head. WM will go through the items you currently have in your kitchen and analyze which ones you can use for beef or fish recipes, and then update

Cognitive Flexibility

Cognitive flexibility (CF) is your ability to be able to look at objects from a different angle, as well as the ability to be able to see other people's points of view [6]. CF also occurs when you think about something in a new way (trying a different solution to a problem, or trying to look at it from a different angle) [6].

Essentially, this executive function allows you to be able to adapt to life's surprises by keeping you on track to being a productive member of society.

Chapter 2 Behavior Self-Regulation

To maintain and reach your goals, you need to have a stable form of self-regulation. Self-regulation in this context refers to the ability for a person to control their actions. Psychologist Kruglanski notes that there are two primary modes of self-regulation: assessment and locomotion [17].

Assessment is the process of "assessing" your goal/task by taking into account all of the possible ways that you could go about doing something (as well as the pros and cons for each method) before you start work on a task [17]. Locomotion is the process of starting your job without an in-depth look at all the ways that you can accomplish it. [17]. Assessors are thinkers, while locomotives are doers [17].

You cannot go through life by only utilizing assessment or locomotion. Kruglanski notes that both assessment and locomotion mostly work separately, but you need both forms of regulation if you want to be successful in reaching your goals. [17]. You always need to plan at least a few things out, and you need to make sure that you execute your goals at some point.

Just because everyone uses both assessment and locomotion, does not mean that they will use each the same way. It is possible for a person to excel in both assessment and locomotion, only excel at one of them, or be horrible at both of them [17].

Assessor And Locomotive Characteristics

Both forms of behavior control share the same characteristics (it is just how they use them that is different!). Those shared characteristics are self-evaluation, how they feel and experience emotions, decisiveness, task completion, internal drive, the ability to make your own choices (autonomy), and self-regulation [17].

Self-regulation is broken down into five further

categories: 1) quality vs. quantity of goals, 2) the number of options looked at to reach goals, 3) how you achieve your goals, 4) inconsistency identification, and, 5) speed of work.[17].

How A Thinker (Assessor) Acts

How does someone who excels at assessment evaluate themselves? Well, thinkers compare themselves to others [17]. They even compare themselves with the person they think others want them to be [17]!

Thinkers may focus on their faults when they fall short and will experience many negative emotions [17]. They will also struggle to make decisions because they want to map out all of their options to see which is the best fit for them[17].

Thinkers will take longer to complete tasks because they want to double check their work to see if they need to make any changes [17]. Thinkers are more likely to be driven by outside forces because they care what other people think of them [17]. A thinker's self-worth will be highly dependent on others praise.

As far as self-regulation goes, thinkers want to produce quality work [17]. They will need to use some forms of locomotor regulation [17]. A thinker cannot just plan out their goals forever; they need to *start* working on their goals for them to see any progress. Otherwise, they will be paralyzed by the number of options they have to complete their task [17].

Being able to spot inconsistencies in your work is key to being able to produce quality results. Thinkers will be better at finding discrepancies in their work because they are worried about being judged for missing them [17].

Lastly, thinkers will move at a slow pace, (unless they have time constraints to worry about) [17]. In summary, thinkers tend to take time to focus on their goals, plan them out, and make sure their work is of high value.

How A Doer (Locomotor) Acts

How does someone who excels at locomotion evaluate themselves? They do not compare themselves with other people, so they can complete more tasks [17]. As a result, they will be happier with themselves and tend to be more optimistic [17].

Doers will make decisions quickly because they are itching to get work done [17]. They will be sure to finish their tasks as they are highly motivated [17]. Doers are driven by their motivation and will not care (as much) what other people are saying about them [17]. A doer wants to be able to complete as many of their goals as possible; they are not concerned with producing imperfect work [17]

Doers allow themselves the bare minimum of choices

and then pick the most efficient way to reach their goal [17]. However, it is not enough to start working on your goals; doers will need some plan (via assessment) to know how they will accomplish them [17].

Inconsistency spotting is not unique to thinkers. Doers also need to be aware of mistakes if they want to produce work that is of good (or passable) quality. However, if checking for errors becomes too time-consuming, doers may settle for "good enough" and continue to their next task [17].

Regulatory Behavior Characteristics Of Procrastinators

Kruglanski and colleagues found that people who are doers multitask, work faster, and abstain from procrastination [16]. Procrastinators will most likely be the complete opposite of these people. Procrastinators should be more likely to be thinkers, work slower, and will be less likely to multitask. Choy and Cheung did find that procrastinators are more likely to be thinkers [2].

But what makes a thinker a procrastinator? It depends on how they perceive time, their emotions, and where they feel pressure is coming from [2].

In 2018, Choy and Cheong researched 196 undergraduates from a Hong Kong university to further understand how these three aspects affected procrastination [2]. Choy and Cheong gave the students a variety of psychological questionnaires, scales, and inventories to see how these concepts changed their behavior [2].

Time

Time is seen as a resource (something that you have a finite amount of) and as a timeline [16]. People who are doers (locomotor based) see time as a resource that needs to be conserved and are more concerned with the future [2]. Thinkers (assessment based) are, therefore, less likely to see time as a limited resource, and are more concerned with the past and the mistakes they have made[2].

Doers want to be able to start and finish as many tasks as they can, so it makes sense that they are aware of how limited their time is; therefore, they will procrastinate less.

People can view a timeline in one of two ways [2]. They can look at what they have done in the past, make choices based on biases, and then stick to what has worked for them in the past [2]. Or, they can look to the future, and base their goals on what they want to be able to achieve [2].

Choy and Cheong found that students who were doers focused both on their past and their futures [2]. Seeing as doers are less likely to procrastinate, they can look at their past mistakes and take corrective actions to make sure they do not repeat them. They are always improving.

Students who were thinkers were focused more on the negativity in their past [2]. Since these students are preoccupied with their past failures, they may be reluctant to try again. Their fear of failure leads them to procrastinate.

Emotion

This 2018 study found that students who were doers were more likely to have positive feelings, and those who were thinkers were more likely to experience negative emotions [2]. People who can get a lot of work done will feel happy about what they have accomplished. Those who do not get a lot of work done will beat themselves up over it.

Internal Vs. External Pressure

A person can view their goal or task outcomes as being pressured through internal or external means [2]. It has been shown that those who mostly base their results on internal pressure will be less likely to procrastinate [2]. And those who base their outcomes on external forces are more likely to avoid procrastination [2]. Choy and Cheong found that doers experienced internal pressure, whereas thinkers experienced external pressure [2].

In other words, those who only look at their goals based on their efforts, desires, and stamina are going to procrastinate less. While those who base the outcome of their goals on what other people may think or how others will view them are going to delay more. These latter individuals could be paralyzed by not being good enough to those around them (friends, parents, teachers, bosses, etc.). Therefore, they procrastinate. These are the thinkers.

Choy and Cheong's study shows that a person bases their procrastination behavior through how they view time, people's emotions, and where and how they feel pressured. How you view your actions in the past, how you see the future, your feelings, and who or what you think influences the control over your situation all affect your behavior and whether or not you will procrastinate. Procrastination is a complex behavior to parse out, but studies like these help us break it down.

Impulsivity

Impulsivity is a behavior that is composed of four distinct characteristics: urgency, premeditation, perseverance, and sensation seeking [27].

Urgency is when one acts hastily when they experience strong, usually negative emotions [27]. Premeditation is, of course, thinking about what you will do before you do it [27]. If one is highly impulsive, then there will be little to no premeditation to their actions.

Perseverance means having the ability to continue

working on a task which is annoying, difficult, or confusing for you to complete [27]. Procrastinators tend not to have the ability to focus on a tedious assignment because it does not stimulate their minds.

This leads us to sensation seeking: being how often you seek out and enjoy new and exciting activities [27]. If someone has been working the same job for a long time, they are more likely to get tired of it and will want to do something else.

Some people have theorized that procrastination and impulsivity are linked [32]. Wu and colleagues set out to find evidence that supported this theory since they could not find any.

In 2016, Wu and colleagues recorded the brain activity of 44 Beijing university students while they participated in choice tasks that gauged their impulsivity [32]. Before they began the tests, students were placed in either a low or high procrastination group [32].

The students had to choose between getting 8 USD immediately, or more money at a later date in time [32]. Students who were in the high procrastination group showed a high level of impulsivity [32]. They became more impulsive when Wu and colleagues told them that they would not receive the money until later and later dates (from 5 days up to a year) [32]. Students in the low procrastination group did not behave in this way [32].

Although this study was small, it is one of the first to link procrastination to impulsivity. This could explain why it is so hard for people who are chronic procrastinators to focus on their tasks. When they are performing a tedious job that will not have any pay off for a long time, they are more likely to be enticed by a more exciting immediate substitute.

Chapter 3 How Thinking Contributes To Procrastination

We have gone over cognitive and behavior modes of regulation and touched briefly on how they relate to procrastination. But what about our thoughts? How does the way we think affect our procrastinatory ways? Luckily, some researchers have determined this was a worthwhile area of study.

Rebetez and colleagues gave 141 French people questionnaires to examine how their procrastination was related to their impulsivity (urgency and perseverance deficits), and intrusive thoughts [27]. These intrusive thoughts consisted of rumination (where one repeatedly thinks about themselves and their experiences for an extended period) and daydreaming (ideas that are not prompted by or related to the task at hand) [27].

One form of rumination is where you play a conversation you had with someone over, and over, and over again in your head, and come up with different ways that you could have responded. Similarly, one could ruminate on how they could have changed their actions to better the outcome of their current situation.

You daydream when you think about how fun it would be to go down to the beach with friends when you are supposed to be writing your term paper.

Rebetez found that people who had a higher tendency to procrastinate also had higher rates of impulsivity, and they also experienced intrusive thoughts to a high degree [27]. If participants procrastinated a lot, then they also tended to ruminate and daydream a lot as well. Procrastinating participants were more likely to be impulsive.

Specifically, if you have high rates of urgency, then you would ruminate more, which would lead to more procrastination [27]. Urgency is when one acts hastily once they experience strong, usually negative emotions [27].

If one tends to react badly to things once they are feeling negative, then it makes sense that those individuals would ruminate more on their situation. They would be taking those negative emotions and funnel them into what they should or could have done better. Spending time on these thoughts allows the person to put off their work.

The converse is also true: those who ruminated more had more urgency and procrastinated to a higher degree [27]. If one is predisposed to contemplating, then they may tend to experience more negative thoughts. These thoughts will lead to negative emotions, which will cause the individual to act hastily/rashly. This person will then want to soothe themselves to feel better, and will further procrastinate on their tasks.

Participants who had a significant lack of perseverance daydreamed more, and therefore had higher rates of procrastination [27]. Those who lacked focus would, of course, be more distracted by things around them. Seeing a new object may lead them to fantasize for an extended period.

The reverse was also true: those who daydreamed a lot lacked perseverance and procrastinated more [27]. Those who are heavy daydreamers cannot stay focused on tedious tasks. Why would they want to do something monotonous, when they could be thinking of all the fun they could be having.

Surprisingly, rumination did not always lead to procrastination [27]. Stewing over their thoughts did not mean that the participants of this study would procrastinate. Rebetez believes that this may be because only rumination of a specific type at a particular time leads to procrastination [27]. More studies will need to be performed to obtain an explanation for this result.

Perhaps people who procrastinate by ruminating and daydreaming so much is not because they are bored or tired of their work. Probably, it is because they are perfectionists. They want everything they do to be perfect. Maybe they are too scared to get started. Perhaps they are afraid that they will fail. Maybe they are scared they will not be perfect.

Perfectionism Can Lead To Burnout

Perfectionism is defined as aiming for error-free work by setting unrealistic standards of performance, and later being extremely critical when the action or behavior is finished [29]. Essentially, a perfectionist is a person who wants everything they think, say and do to be perfect.

Trying to be perfect all of the time can be draining. It can become so exhausting that people do not care what happens anymore. In other words, they are experiencing burnout. Burnout occurs when you experience emotional exhaustion, depersonalize (become cynical and withdraw from others), and stop evaluating your competence or accomplishments [13].

The interplay between demands (workload) and resources (social support) lead to burnout [13]. You are heading towards burnout if the demands in your life outweigh your resources [13]. To avoid burnout, you need to make sure that your demands and resources are relatively even. Be sure to take time to recharge if you feel yourself heading towards burnout.

Currently, perfectionism is seen as being composed of two sides, perfectionistic strivings and perfectionistic concerns [13]. Perfectionistic strivings consist of wanting to aim for perfection, or having extremely high standards for oneself [13]. Perfectionistic concerns are those aspects that carry negative connotations; worries about failing, being judged and feeling like you cannot live up to your standards [13].

There have been hundreds of studies that have analyzed the relationships between perfectionism and burnout. In 2016, Hill and Curran performed a meta-analysis of 43 of them to distill the relationship between perfectionism and burnout into one paper [13] Their results were what you would expect.

They found that perfectionistic strivings had little to no relationship with burnout or its symptoms [13]. Just wanting to aim for perfection is not in and of itself bad. Nor is having high standards for yourself. This part of perfectionism can be a good motivator. No one wants to produce inferior work.

By setting high standards for yourself, you will aim to do the best that you can on whatever you set your sights to. Burnout has little chance of affecting you via perfectionistic strivings alone. Shooting for the best that you can be will still give you a favorable outcome.

It will not be perfect, but it will be better than a lot of other people's work!

However, we have seen that perfectionism is not single-sided. And with every good side, there is a bad side. Here, the bad is perfectionistic concerns.

Hill and Curran found that perfectionistic concerns have a medium to a large relationship with burnout and its symptoms [13]. This is not surprising since this facet contains all of the negatives of procrastination. Wanting to be perfect, but being terrified of failing. Doing your best, but in the back of your mind, you are wondering if everyone is judging you as harshly as you are judging yourself. You fear that you will be unable to be the best you *know* you can be.

Having these concerns will, of course, inevitably lead to burnout. There are demands from those around you at work, school, or home. Additionally, you have internal orders telling you to do better. To be better.

These demands will tax you to the point where you cannot deal with anybody or anything anymore.

You detach from your resources, your social net. Perhaps you feel that there is no way they could understand what you are going through. Eventually, you will stop seeing how amazing your accomplishments are. Burnout is inevitable.

Not everything you do has to be perfect. Everything you do daily does not need to be held up to the high standard you think it does. Sometimes good enough is perfect.

Chapter 4 Personality And Procrastination – Is It Genetics?

Now you may be thinking, is procrastination a habit I picked up through my environment or did it come from my genetics? How would we even go about testing this? Every person is different, albeit families are similar, so how would this be studied? The answer? Twins.

Why twins? Well, twin studies are valuable because they allow us to compare persons who have identical or very similar DNA. If you haven't taken a biology class in a while, here is a quick refresher:

DNA contains the genetic code of all aspects of life. DNA encodes genes. Each person has two copies of every single gene in their body. These genes code for functional proteins.

Now back to the twins.

Twin Studies

Identical twins share 100% of their DNA. While fraternal twins share about 50% of their DNA. [11]. Generally, twins are raised in the same home (environment), so any encountered differences can easily be pinned down to genetics or environment [11].

In 2014, Daniel E. Gustavson published a study on the relationship between procrastination, impulsivity, and goal-management [11].

Previous studies showed that procrastination is linked to impulsivity [11]. If a person is likely to be impulsive, then they are also expected to be procrastinators. The reverse is true as well; those who are more likely to be procrastinators are more likely to be impulsive.

Both procrastination and being impulsive seem to affect a person's ability to reach their goals;

procrastinating will lead to a delay of the tasks that you need to achieve your goals, and being impulsive means that you will be unable to resist distracting temptations [11]. These problems are caused by a deficit in executive functions (inhibitory control and working memory), as well as regulatory functions (intrinsic motivation, self-regulation, as well as decisiveness, to name a few).

To examine the link between procrastination and being impulsive even further, Gustavson analyzed questionnaires that 181 identical and 166 fraternal twins took on procrastination, impulsivity, and goal failures to see how all of these behaviors were related [11]. If these traits are linked, then this should easily be shown since each twin pair would have similar answers.

The results indicated that procrastination was heritable, and both procrastination and impulsivity play a role in how goals are managed [11].

Procrastination is a trait that is "in your genes." Both procrastination and impulsivity effect how you complete your goals.

Having studies done that show that procrastination and impulsivity affect how a person reaches their goals may seem like "common sense" to you. But, if we have data that supports "common sense" notions like these, it will make it easier for society to see that (to some extent) procrastination and impulsivity cannot be helped. "Common sense" studies like this one may help us understand more complicated issues in the future.

Gustavson's study is important because it is one of the first to investigate the role between procrastination and impulsivity at the subconscious level [11]. Although this genetic and behavior study gives us greater insight into procrastinations heritability, it does not delve deep enough into exploring how these traits are expressed. To do that, we need to investigate deeper.

One gene that has been indicated in helping regulate impulsive behavior is COMT [4]. Since Gustavson found that procrastination is correlated to impulsive behavior, a good next step would be to see if the COMT gene plays any role in procrastination.

The Role Of COMT In Procrastination

COMT is a protein expressed in neurons (brain cells). Neurons send signals to each other to regulate our actions. These signals are released from one neuron and then bind to receptors on another neuron. This message is relayed from neuron to neuron until its final destination is reached. When it arrives, the signal is converted, and we execute an action or behavior.

One of the signals involved in regulating attention, cognition, and emotions is dopamine [5]. COMT is a gene that helps control the level of dopamine between neurons [4], so there is a good chance that COMT will play a role in regulating procrastination behavior.

One version of the COMT gene, "comt", contains a mutation that makes the protein less effective at regulating dopamine [5]. People who have the "comt" gene will have higher levels of dopamine outside of their neurons [5].

Low levels of dopamine have been tied to impulsive behavior [5]. People who have the "COMT" gene are more likely to be spontaneous, while people who have the "comt" gene will not be as spontaneous [5]. Remember, being unable to inhibit impulsive behavior means you might have some impairment in your executive functions.

To recap, people who have the standard "COMT" gene will have less dopamine outside of their neurons. People who have the mutated "comt" gene will have more dopamine outside of their neurons. Those people who have the "comt" genes should be less impulsive than those who have the "COMT" gene.

Di Nocera decided to study the role of the COMT genes in procrastination after reviewing the work Gustavson did in 2014 that linked impulsivity to procrastination [5].

Di Nocera had 20 university students complete questionnaires and write a summary of an academic article in a Google Document which had an eight-day deadline [5]. Researchers were able to see how much time each of the students spent on their written assignment. [5]. The students' saliva was also collected to analyze which type of the COMT gene they had [5]. Again, remember that everybody has *two* copies of every gene.

He found that students who had two copies of the mutated 'comt" gene, and those that had one copy each of the normal "COMT" and mutated "comt" gene, were more likely to start and finish their assigned task; [5]. Students who had two copies of the normal "COMT" gene were more likely to procrastinate on their assignment [5].

It is likely that if you have one, or two, of the mutated "comt" genes that you are less likely to procrastinate. If you have two copies of the normal "COMT" gene, then you are more likely to procrastinate.

The students who have two copies of the normal "COMT" gene might have trouble with their executive functioning. They may have had a hard time ignoring distractions around them, and a hard time focusing on the task on hand.

Does Serotonin Play A Role In Procrastination?

Another signal that has been linked to impulsivity is serotonin [1] [5]. When serotonin levels are low, an individual tends to be more impulsive [5].

One of the genes that helps regulate serotonin is SLC6A4 [1] [5]. There are also two types of this gene, one is the "long" gene, and the other is the "short" gene [1] [5]. People who have the "long" gene have less serotonin outside of their neurons [5]. People who have the "long" gene should be more impulsive then. Those who have the "short" gene have more serotonin outside of their neurons [5]. People who have the "short" gene should not be very impulsive.

In the same 2017 study, Di Nocera and colleagues looked at which version of the serotonin gene the students who took part in the experiment had [5].

However, they found no relationship between students who had either the "long" gene or "short" gene and procrastination [5]. It seems that this particular serotonin gene does not play a role in impulsive behavior.

Takeaways

Procrastination *is* in your genes!

Procrastination and impulsiveness effect how you complete your goals.

People who have two copies of the normal "COMT" version of the COMT gene are more likely to procrastinate. People who have two copies of the mutated "comt" gene, or one mutated "comt" and one "COMT" gene will not procrastinate as much.

The serotonin gene SLC6A4 does not affect procrastination.

Although this study only had 20 students, these results are promising. Linking the COMT gene with procrastination is an essential first step. Di Nocera's experiment was the first to investigate the role specific genes might play in procrastination. Hopefully, more studies that examine this relationship (and perhaps even other serotonin genes) will be published in the future!

Chapter 5 Changing Your Brain

At this point, you might be thinking: "Ok, so I know I'm a procrastinator now. It probably is a result of my genetics, and how I am hardwired to approach the world. So, there's nothing that I can do to change my procrastinating ways; is there?"

Wrong!

Your brain is always changing! Just because you are predisposed to procrastinate, or because you have been a procrastinator for so long you can't see yourself being anything else, does not mean all hope is lost! It may be hard to get started, but once you have the right tools in your kit, you will be able to start chipping away at your procrastination habits!

Your Changing Brain

In a 2009 interview, Dr. Bryan Kolb said, "Brain

development is very rapid in the womb and continues at an accelerated rate in the first two to three years in particular. Although the sculpting of the brain activity continues for the next 20 years or more, early life experiences will affect your responses throughout life" [14].

The most significant changes to our brain development occur before we are even aware of it! Our early years on this earth set the tone for how we will respond to everything around us. We are then further shaped and changed by brain growth that happens from preschool age to our mid-twenties.

Afraid that it is too late for you to change since you are older than 25? Fear not! Dr. Kolb continues: "the brain remains 'plastic' throughout life" [14]. This is great news! Our brains remain "plastic" (malleable) for our entire lives! This means that we can change the bad habits that have stuck with us since childhood and replace them with new and improved ones.

In fact, Dr. Kolb says that "anything that changes your brain, changes who you will be. Your brain is not just a product of your genes; it's sculpted by a lifetime of experiences. Experience alters brain activity, which changes gene expression" [14]. We are more than just our genes. Both good and bad experiences help shape who we are down to the molecular level.

But it is not just our experiences that can alter our brains. Our behaviors also affect them. Dr. Kolb concludes, "Any behavioral changes you see reflect alterations in the brain. The opposite is also true: behavior can change the brain"[14]. So, our gene expression changes our behavior, and our behavior changes our gene expression.

This may seem like circular reasoning, and in some ways it is. BUT this means that we can break this circle by forcing ourselves to change our habits. Changing habits is never easy (as anyone who has tried sticking to a diet, or attempted to maintain a gym schedule can attain). However, once we get over the hurdle, set new habits in motion, and stick with them, our gene expressions will change to make it easier for us to replace the old with the new.

How do you reach the point where you can just "do it"? If it is late in the day, you're probably thinking, I'll do it tomorrow. Perhaps you are reading this in the middle of the week, and thinking: "It's better to start change at the beginning of the week, so I'll hold off until Sunday or Monday."

No!

Getting Started Creates The Right Mood!

Get started now! Go do something that you have been putting off! Throw the trash on your table away. Go through the growing pile of mail that has been sitting on your desk for the past week or two. Put away your clean laundry. Sweep the floor. Do something you have been putting off right now and then come back.

Did you do it? Great! Don't you feel better already? That rewarding feeling comes from dopamine; the "feel good" hormone. When dopamine is released, you are rewarded with a satisfied feeling for a job well done.

In 2010, Dr. Herd wrote, "dopamine release in itself serves to, lock' attention on the item, task, or concept currently being attended to or represented"[12]. In other words, dopamine will be released every time you complete a task. Remembering this feeling will help you stay motivated in all that you have to do. And all because you decided to get started tackling your list!

There is a downside though. As you become used to doing something successfully repeatedly, the impact of dopamine's' release begins to wear off [12]. You will then feel compelled to seek out new/other tasks that you can complete to experience that rush of dopamine again [12]. Over the long term, you will get many things done! One success will lead to another, which will lead to another.

Costs And Consequences

Maybe none of this has convinced you. Perhaps you think it's still ok to procrastinate because you perform well under pressure. Or, you think "I have been procrastinating my whole life. It's probably in my genes anyway, so why should I change now?"

You need to think about the consequences. Visualizing the costs might help stop you from procrastinating. Here are a few examples.

Waiting Until The Last Minute In School

You are assigned a paper at the beginning of the term that will be due at the end. It is a big paper, and it is worth a good chunk of your grade. If you put off researching, outlining, and writing the paper until the last few weeks, or even the *final* week, you will be rushing to finish it.

While you are busy writing your paper, studying for your other classes' finals falls to the wayside. You write as much as you can to fill the page requirement and turn in your paper. Next, you hurriedly study for each final just hours before you have them.

A week later you get your results and see that you received a passing grade, "C", on your paper, and your final grades in your other classes weren't too much better.

Your failure to study effectively, plan out and write your essay over the term, and being exhausted while taking your finals has resulted in you just barely passing all of your classes. Procrastinating on one portion of your school work has affected all of it.

Putting Off Your Finances

There are many ways that you could procrastinate on your finances. Most, if not all, of them, have ill effects on your financial stability. Financial situations vary in a lot of ways, but one thing that everyone has in common is a budget.

Every household should have a budget. A record of income coming in, and deducted expenses. Those who do not have a budget are at risk of overspending. They may want to start one, but think it is too hard to draw up. Or maybe, they keep saying they will get to it tomorrow. But tomorrow keeps being pushed back.

They don't have a written record of their bills but keep a mental tally going. With everything that you have going on in your life, it can be extremely easy to forget to pay a bill or two. Forgetting to pay these bills can result in late fees and increases in interest rates on credit cards. Now you have even less money to spend on leisure.

People also procrastinate on saving for retirement. They may think they are too young to start saving now or they do not make enough money to make it worthwhile. Savings keep getting put off year after year until it becomes too daunting to start. Once you do start saving for retirement, you won't be able to save enough in time to truly enjoy your golden years. You will need to continue working to pay for all of your needs.

Health On Hiatus

If you are prone to procrastinating, you will most likely feel guilty about it. This might lead to you beating yourself up over it, ruminating on it, and trying to cope with your resulting feelings in inefficient ways (poor eating habits, substance abuse, etc.). These are known as "maladaptive coping" strategies (harmful coping strategies), and they are linked to stress caused by procrastination[28].

A 2015 study found that procrastination is linked to a variety of health problems, including headaches, digestive issues, colds, flu, and insomnia [28]. Self-harming thoughts and ruminating on all the ways that you have messed up due to procrastination often occur at night while you are lying in bed. That is when there is the least amount of distractions that can draw us away from our thoughts. Rumination at bedtime could potentially lead to insomnia.

Eating poorly and abusing drugs and alcohol can lead to a weakened immune system. The body does not have the correct amount of nutrients to function effectively, which may cause digestive issues. Your body is also not as prepared to fight infections, leading you to get sick more often. Chronic stress has been shown to lead to the worsening of sicknesses and diseases because it helps disrupt the body's ability to keep inflammation in check [28].

When you are sick, you often do not feel like performing the tasks that you need to do, not to mention the ones that you don't want to do. Being sick pushes completion of these tasks even further away, which will also weigh on you.

Procrastination can also occur *after* you have been diagnosed with a disease. That same 2015 study found that those individuals who were diagnosed with hypertension and cardiovascular disease often turn to harmful coping behaviors to deal with the stress of the illness [28]. These destructive behaviors can lead to a delay in treatment, which further exacerbates the disorders. Putting off treatment could lead to even more illnesses or even death.

Chapter 6 Improving (Slowly)

You now know that you can change your behavior. You know that just starting will release dopamine to encourage you to keep going. You have thought about the consequences of procrastinating, and are ready to change.

It may feel like a good idea to change all of your procrastination habits at once. Don't do that! Although it is a well-intentioned plan, changing too many things at once will result in failure. It will be too hard to maintain all of the changes that you want to start with. Seeing this, you may feel like giving up and think that you should learn to live with your procrastinating self.

Instead, you should try small changes, as exemplified by Dr. BJ Fogg. Dr. Fogg is a prominent behavior scientist who developed the Fogg Behavior Model (FBM) in 2007 [8]. The FBM states that behavior occurs when motivation, ability, and a prompt (cue, or trigger) align at the same time [8]. In other words, you need to be able to want to do something, have the skills to do it, and need to be reminded to perform the behavior in order for it to be executed.

Dr. Fogg states, "One of the best ways to get people to do a behavior in the long term is to build their confidence and ability through baby steps...It sounds trivial, but it's not. Baby steps are super powerful. It's a way to help people continue to do harder and harder behaviors" [8]. If you start with baby steps, you are more likely to succeed. These successes will lead to an increase in motivation. A person is more likely to do something if they know that they will be able to accomplish it beforehand.

Starting with baby steps also ensures that you will stick with your new habits. If you want to make a behavior automatic, then consistency is key! Repeating things over and over and over helps build up muscle memory. Once you have that muscle memory, you will be compelled to do that task! By continuing to stick with your baby steps, you are ensuring that this new behavior will stay with you as you grow old.

Dr. Fogg continues, "If you start people out doing something easy and if they feel successful doing that thing they're much more likely to do it again because that behavior becomes easier to do" [8]. Simple enough, right? Small victories will improve your mood (you will get that rush of dopamine), and you will want to experience that feeling again.

If you continue making these small habits, you will become addicted to the feeling of accomplishment. This will make you want to keep doing behaviors that will benefit you. You will be crushing your goals before you know it!

However, for you to transform your bad habits into good ones, you need the new pattern to be reliable [9]. That is, the new practice must be something that you can keep up with day in and day out. Small, stable habits are easier to maintain. If you try to change too much too fast, you are at risk of dropping those new habits altogether and returning to your old ways.

"Slow And Steady Wins The Race."

Changing your behavior slowly at first may seem annoyingly slow, but if you want to see improvement in your life, you need to do it this way. Small changes are easier to keep, easier to maintain, and the easiest to fit into your day to day life.

One goal that a lot of people have is to eat healthier. Many people put it off because they see it as "too hard to do" or "too expensive". They say that they will start at the beginning of the week. But when Monday arrives, they are reluctant to start. Or a party might come up, and they don't want to be the only one not enjoying treats. So, they push it back to the start of next month.

When the new month arrives, they are ready to make as many changes as possible to make up for the time they lost. However, this can be very detrimental to your ability to continue your new habits. Don't believe it? Well, then it is time for another example.

Let's pretend that a person named Mary wants to improve her diet. As of right now, most days she skips breakfast and eats a large lunch that she buys from work. When she gets home, she orders delivery. The days that she does not buy or order out, she brings unhealthy pre-packaged food from home. She is tired of living like this, so she decides to make some drastic changes. But maintaining those drastic changes will be harder than she thought.

Big Changes - Change Everything Right Now!!!

Mary makes some drastic decisions to improve her life. She decides to start a new chapter in her life, and to do that; she needs to change everything right now.

Mary goes to her cupboards and tosses everything she has into the garbage. Then, she goes to the local grocer and buys a variety of fresh fruit and vegetables (all organic of course). She also decides to buy some lean cuts of meat to have some protein.

After her shopping trip, she comes home, washes all of the produce, cuts it up, bags it, and proceeds to cook the meat. Exhausted, and not looking forward to just eating "rabbit food" tonight, she rummages around in the bin looking for some of her favorite "bad" snacks to go along with some of the meat.

In the morning, she grabs the lunch she prepped yesterday, along with a banana for breakfast and heads out to work. At first, everything is going fine, and Mary feels better now that she has eaten breakfast for the first time in months. "I could get used to this", she tells herself.

When lunchtime rolls around, Mary's enthusiasm has

waned as she remembers what she brought for lunch: "rabbit food". She begrudgingly eats it. Mary finds herself daydreaming about all of the food that she threw out the day before, as well as the lunches she so desperately misses.

At the end of the workday, she goes home, starving. Woozily, she orders take out from her couch and scarfs most of it down before she realizes she has overeaten. Putting the leftovers away, she promises herself that she will be better tomorrow.

The next morning arrives, and she grabs her banana and "rabbit food". It is a similar day as the one before it. Again, when she gets home, she scarfs down the remainder of last night's meal. She tries to continue to eat healthy for the rest of the week but falls back onto her old habits. She finds it too hard and too frustrating for her to keep up with her new way of life.

Mary has tried to change too much too fast, and as a

result, she has regressed to her old habits. (Although some of the new habits she initiated were on the right track – the banana!).

It is easy enough for anyone to do what she did because we all want to see changes in our lives. However, small changes, over a more extended period are easier to maintain.

Now let us look and see what would happen if Mary applied Dr. Fogg's behavior method.

Small Changes – Adjust As Needed

Mary decides that it is time to start taking control of her life. She does some research and learns about the FBM. Thinking that this will help her with her goals of eating better, Mary decides to try this method out for a while. So, she starts to make slow, deliberate changes.

Like before, Mary goes to her cupboards, but this time she is more selective with what she throws away. The unhealthiest of her unhealthy snacks are the ones that find a new home in the trash. Fewer tempting snacks are in the house, and now they are a tad bit healthier. She then goes to the grocer and picks up some bananas.

The next day she eats the banana for breakfast and finds that she feels better than she has in a long time. She continues to eat the banana for breakfast for the rest of the month and is surprised to discover that she is gradually feeling better. After a while, eating the banana is automatic, and she no longer has to remind herself to eat it regularly.

The second small change she decides to make is regarding her dinners. When she next goes to the grocer, she picks out some (relatively) healthy single serve dinners. She is now able to focus on making this change every night because she has already adapted to the one she made in regards to breakfast. In time, she no longer needs to remember to forego takeout at dinner.

Thirdly, she decides to start changing her lunch habits. At lunchtime, instead of buying a massive meal like she usually does, she orders a cheeseburger and diet soda. This habit also becomes automatic, which further increases her ability to make more changes. (Such as switching the diet soda to water!) The changes are becoming easier and easier for her to make.

Mary finds that she can actually keep this routine up. Slip-ups occur now and then, but they don't drag her down (as they did in the previous example). Slowly, she starts making more changes, and she can keep up with them.

By implementing Dr. Foggs Behavior Model, Mary was able to make significant changes in her life through small actions. Maybe you have eating habits that are similar to Mary's, but you think the changes she made are too drastic. That is ok! You can make even smaller changes than she did.

Instead of buying single serve meals for dinner, you can order healthier items at your favorite fast food place. Instead of foregoing buying combination meals at lunch, you can start buying combos that do not include as much food. Then you can begin switching over from regular soda to diet soda. Eventually, you could substitute tea for the diet soda. Finally, you can replace the tea with water.

Make the smallest change that you can reasonably make, and see how your behavior improves from there!

The Compound Effect – How The Little Things Add Up

Are all of these small changes even going to make a difference? Yes, they will! And to see how, we must return to Dr. Fogg.

In 2012, Dr. Fogg presented a talk on tiny habits at a TED talk event (TEDxFremont) [9]. During his speech, he said there are two main ways that you can make lasting behavior change: 1) changing your environment, and, 2) make tiny behavior changes (tiny habits) [9]. People can improve their environment, but only to a certain degree. That leaves us with tiny habits.

But, we do not want to design these habits with our intended outcomes in mind; we want to develop them with the behaviors that we can repeatedly make to reach our intended goal [9]. By putting your efforts into the behaviors needed to achieve your end goal, you are setting yourself up for success.

Focusing on the outcome you want to achieve can be too daunting. Thinking about how far you are from where you want to be can be very discouraging and may cause you to slip up. Looking at the distance you have to go puts you at a higher risk of abandoning your goals altogether before you even try to start reaching them.

By focusing only on the behaviors that will lead to your desired end goals, you are more likely to reach them. Incorporating small behaviors into your daily life is easy, and it is something that almost everyone can do. The ease of integrating new habits into your everyday life dramatically increases the chances that you will reach your end goal.

According to Dr. Fogg, behaviors are caused when three things occur at the same time: motivation, ability, and a prompt (or trigger) [9]. Motivation and ability are pretty self-explanatory, but how will a prompt help you induce a new behavior?

New behaviors will occur if you tie them to an existing action that happens every day at a set frequency [9]. By tying them together, you will be sure to enact the new behavior.

Dr. Fogg says that the correct way to implement tiny habits into your life is by using this formula:

After I (existing habit), I will (new tiny behavior). [9]

He has used this formula to help introduce pushups into his daily life. "After I pee, I will do two pushups" [9]. Doing pushups is a great way to make sure you are maintaining your upper body strength.

Dr. Fogg could have decided to perform two pushups after every time he used the facilities because: 1) he probably did not have too much motivation to do them, 2) he was able to do two pushups, and 3) going to the restroom was something that he reliably did every day with a similar frequency day to day.

By tying pushups to peeing, he was able to fit multiple small workouts into his day every single day. As two pushups became more comfortable for him, he increased the number of pushups from 2 to 5, then to 8, and finally stopped at 10 to 12 [9]. (If you want a more natural way to incorporate this habit, you could start at one push up, move on to 2, then 3, etc.).

Now every day he does at least 50 pushups. He did not make this change quickly either; it took him about a year to go from doing two pushups after every time he peed to doing 10 to 12 [9]. Over time, his tiny habit became easier, so he added more to it to benefit himself.

The key to keeping up these small behavioral changes is to perform tiny celebrations after you do them [9].

Simple things like saying "I'm awesome!" while pumping your fists in the air, or doing a little dance after you perform the new behavior are some of the ways Dr. Fogg says you can celebrate [9]. Like the tiny habits that you are creating, you want the celebrations to be tiny as well. By pairing tiny habits with tiny celebrations, you are ensuring that those tiny habits will become fun and second nature to you.

These tiny behaviors can also be used to achieve significant outcomes. Dr. Fogg himself said he "created many, many, many, many, many tiny habits" over a year to aid in his weight loss; he ended up losing 20 pounds in a year! [9].

He did not say what these tiny habits were, but here are some he probably implemented. (If anything, you should feel free to try them yourself!).

Substitute diet soda for regular soda. Complete five jumping jacks during commercials while watching tv.

Drink a glass of water before a meal. Park as far from the store entrance as you can. Stand up, stretch, and then walk around for 2-minutes after sitting at a computer for an hour.

Here are some other tiny habits you could start doing yourself throughout the day to better your life.

Morning Tiny Habits

After I hear my alarm go off, I will open my eyes for 10 seconds.

After I get out of bed, I will make my bed.

After I brush my teeth, I will floss one tooth [9].

After I make coffee/tea, I will take my pills/vitamins.

After I eat breakfast, I will feed my pets.

After I get to work, I will take one flight of stairs.

Afternoon/Evening Tiny Habits

After I eat lunch, I will take a 3-minute walk.

After I respond to an email, I will do one squat.

After I eat my snack, I will take a 1-minute walk.

After I get home, I will hang my keys/put them by the door.

After I collect the mail, I will sort through it.

After I pick up the kids, I will tell them I love them.

Night Tiny Habits

After I eat dinner, I will wash my plate/silverware.

After I watch 25 minutes of tv, I will do three sit-ups.

After I walk the dog, I will refill his food and water.

After I lock the door, I will check my schedule for the next day.

After I brush my teeth, I will floss one tooth [9].

After I get into bed, I will not touch my phone.

Student Specific Tiny Habits

After I enter class, I will not check my phone.

After I get an assignment, I will put it in my calendar.

After I finish class, I will review my notes.

After I eat, I will read one page of the assigned reading.

After I study for 50-minutes, I will walk for 10-minutes.

After I return home, I will review my notes again.

Implementing these tiny habits, or some like these can help make significant changes in your life!

How Building Momentum Helps

Now you might be asking yourself, "How will I be able to build the momentum to accomplish everything that I have been putting off? I'll never be able to do everything that I want to do. Taking baby steps will never get me to where I want to go." Yes, you will! And, yes, they can!

You need to obtain the right momentum, and you will eventually cruise through all of your tasks! Once again, we will return to Dr. Fogg and his behavior model.

Dr. Fogg developed an equation to explain his behavior model, B=MAP; where B is behavior, M is motivation, A is ability, and P is prompt [8]. You can think of motivation as the *momentum* that you need to start your behavior. Ability is how skillful you are at something. And the prompt is a behavior that you already do with some frequency. Difficult tasks will require greater motivation than more manageable tasks.

Motivation and ability are tied together. If you have more motivation to do something, then you can afford not to have as much ability to perform the task. The reverse is true as well; having high ability to perform a task means that you can afford to have lower motivation to do it. Both of these scenarios assume that the new behavior you want to enact is tied to the prompt (old behavior). The old behavior will help "jumpstart" your behavior.

After you make progress via baby steps, your motivation, or your **momentum**, will significantly increase. There will come the point where you reach a "springboard moment" [8]. The "springboard moment" occurs after you have completed a lot of baby steps and feel like you can do harder and harder things [8]. If you accomplish a lot of tasks that you once felt were impossible, then you will have increased motivation (momentum) to complete even harder tasks!

Once people hit their "springboard moment," they can obtain "success momentum"[8]. People will start performing harder and harder tasks because the fear that they had before has been transformed into hope [8]. The fear of failure is something that holds many people back.

But, through many tiny successes, people realize that they can do this. And if they miss a day or two (like they may have with the tiny habits), then it is not the end of the world. They now know that they have the ability (or the potential ability) to accomplish great things.

Once you have greater motivation (momentum) and greater ability, then you will be able to perform greater amounts of behaviors which will help you achieve your goals.

Building Towards A Marathon With Momentum

For instance, let's say you want to run a marathon. If you decide not to break that goal down, then it seems incredibly daunting. You will have no motivation, and no ability to run one [9]. Instead, if you start with the tiny habit of walking outside and back in, you are more likely to follow through with it [9].

Walking in and out of your house is a good baby step to start with. After a while of doing that, you can start increasing the difficulty of your tiny habits. Here is one way that you could do this.

Walk the length of your house. Walk around your home. Walk to the next house and back. Increasingly increase the number of houses you walk down to and back from. Gradually, you can work up to walking around your block. Then you can start implementing 5 seconds of jogging between stretches of walking around the block.

Incrementally, you will increase the amount of time you jog until you can jog around the block. After that, you can work in snippets of running in between your jogging. Next, you could break up a mile by alternating between walking, jogging, and running. If this seems hard, you can add in even more baby steps until you can run for a full mile.

At some point, you will reach your "springboard moment", and you will actively train for a longer period every day. The anxiety you once had about starting at all has now diminished, and you will be determined to work your way up to 26.2 miles. "Success momentum" will kick in, and before you know it, you will be completing your first marathon!

A Momentum Metaphor

Another way to visualize how the building of momentum will help you is to think of a snowball on the top of an extremely steep hill.

Think of yourself as this extremely tiny snowball. You have not had much motivation to change any of your destructive procrastination habits. But all of that is about to change. You are going to start performing one tiny habit a day.

This tiny habit is the smallest amount of momentum that is needed to push the tiny snowball down the steep hill. Just a slight push is all that is required to set it off.

For a long time, the snowball will pick up minuscule amounts of snow. In the same way, your implementation of that one tiny habit will not seem like it is worth the effort.

After some time, the tiny snowball will begin to grow. The change will be barely noticeable, but it will be there. In the same vein, by performing that tiny habit over and over, your momentum will increase. You will be looking forward to completing your tiny habit. In fact, you may even feel sad when you do not get the chance to implement it on a busy day.

Part way down the hill, the snowball begins picking up greater and greater momentum, and, greater and greater amounts of snow. Similarly, you will start to incorporate more and more tiny habits into your day.

Halfway down the hill, the snowball now has so much momentum, that it is gaining in size faster than ever before. Soon, it will become unstoppable. It will continue to roll down the hill, crushing everything in its path.

After a few months, you will be at the same place as this snowball. You will have so much momentum, so much energy, that you will take on harder and harder habits. You will be crushing all of the obstacles in your way, and it all started with that single tiny habit.

Creating new habits can be scary, but changing them slowly over time will help you be the person that you want to be. Here are two quotes from Dr. Fogg that sum up his views quite succinctly:

"Look at your lives. Look at what you want to change; break it down to tiny behaviors and put them in the right spot. The right spot is after something you're already doing" [9].

"When you know how to create tiny habits, you can change your life forever" [9].

Chapter 7 The Right Habits

The Power In Taking Responsibility For Your Actions

To take control of your life, you need to take responsibility for your actions. You cannot lay the blame on others for the way you behave, the way you act, or the way you speak. Not only is that childish, but it is also self-detrimental.

Many of us know of at least one person who has said to us "look what you made me do!" That sense of powerlessness that washes over you destroys your self-esteem and affects your later interactions with that person. You will then step on eggshells around them, or you will try and convince them why they are wrong. Usually, that ends in disaster.

If you become like that person, you are admitting that you have no sense of self: no self-control, nor self-worth, or even self-confidence. Being that person gives you an easy out to do or say whatever you want. This could lead to some potentially dangerous situations for you and others.

But, taking responsibility for your actions frees you from all of that. When you get in an argument with someone and feel like saying "look what you made me do!", take a moment and think about why you feel that way. What is bringing you down? What are the issues you need to resolve?

By stepping back and taking a look at how you think, feel, act, and what you do, you are taking power back for yourself. Assessing what you do, why you do it, and how you can change will bring a great sense of relief to you.

No matter what your reason is for procrastinating, you have to look at why you do it, how you do it, and how you can fix it. As the saying goes, admitting you have a problem is the first step. Once you admit that to yourself, you will feel a sense of relief wash over you. You will feel powerful in knowing that no one is responsible for you but you. It is your life. You need to make the changes to shape it to what you want it to be.

To Manage Something, You Must First Measure It

Now that you have admitted that only you are responsible for you, you can begin changing. But, before you start modifying your habits, you need to assess your current state.

Do you want to change your weight? The first step is figuring out how much you weigh. Then you need to go to a doctor and assess any underlying issues.

Have you been putting off looking at your finances? As painful as it may be, you need to take a hard look at how much debt you have versus income. From there you can start researching different ways to better your situation.

Whatever the habit is that you want to change you have to figure out why you are putting off bettering yourself. You cannot make your situation better until you take a hard look at what it is you have to change. You cannot actively fix anything unless you know what state it is currently in.

Once you figure out why you are putting things off, you can then start to fix them. You can then start making new plans and habits that will get you to where you want to go.

Put Success On Autopilot By Establishing Good Habits – The Can Approach

But how can you ensure that you will stick to your habits? How can you make the right habits easy enough to hold to so that you can achieve all of your goals? Isn't there a way you can automate your habits?

There is a way that will help you get started, and you do not need massive amounts of willpower to use it! What is it you ask? It is the CAN approach.

Wansink developed the CAN approach to change people's eating behavior [31]. CAN stands for Convenient, Attractive, Normal [31]. Wansink found when individuals used his approach, they were able to make healthier choices far easier than when they tried to make those same choices by willpower alone [31]. This method sounds great, but is it too good to be true?

The CAN approach uses three simple points to help you change your eating behavior. First, to improve your eating behaviors, you need to make sure that your new habits are physically or cognitively *convenient* [31]. Second, the new habit must be comparatively or absolutely *attractive* [31]. Lastly, your new habits must be actually (or perceived) to be more *normal* than the old ways [31].

Making something cognitively attractive is as simple as changing the defaults [31]. Wansink explains that changing the default drink in a combo meal to water automatically makes it convenient to drink less soda and more water [31]. Fast food places are not going to be changing this default anytime soon. However, you can!

If you find that you cannot give up your soda habit at home, that's ok! You can make it more convenient for yourself to default to water. Put the soda in the back of the fridge and a jug of water in the front. Knowing that you have to move multiple food items out of the way to retrieve your soda means that you are less likely to reach for it. Now drinking soda is less *convenient* than drinking water.

Because the water is in front of the fridge, you are more likely to drink it. (To make drinking water even more compelling, you could keep it in a jug that has a fancy print or character you like, i.e., make it more attractive). Keeping a water jug in the front of your fridge will also make you start perceiving water as the normal option.

Though he did not test beverages, Wansink found that when healthy food was put on the middle shelf of a refrigerator at home, people tended to choose that over unhealthy food [31]. Those same people even saw healthy food as being more normal to take [31]. Putting healthy beverages like water on those shelves would undoubtedly make them more normal to drink as well!

That is how the CAN method can help you drink more water at home.

Skeptical that this method will work for you? Well implementing this method led to children eating more fruit at school! In 2009, Schools in New York were having trouble getting students to eat fruit; they wanted to increase the amount of fruit that students ate by just 5% [31]. Those schools implemented the CAN approach to try and reach that small goal of 5%.

First, they made the fruit more convenient to take by moving it from an out of the way area to a more heavily trafficked part of the line [31]. Next, the fruit was made more attractive by placing it in various bowls (before they were located underneath a sneeze guard) [31]. Lastly, the fruit became more normal to take because it had been moved from an out of the way place in a drab location, to an area nearer the students and in a more attractive bowl [31].

Over the course of the semester, the schools found that fruit sales increased 103% over the previous term! [31]. By making simple changes, New York schools were able to get picky children to significantly increase their fruit intake. If this method can work for children, then it can certainly work for you!

Even though Wansink developed this approach to

change eating behaviors, that does not mean you can use it in other areas of your life!

Are you avoiding workouts? You can use the CAN method to help you there too! Say you want to start working out once you get home from work. To make that more convenient, you can lay your workout gear out on a chair that you see as soon as you walk in the door.

Making exercising more attractive is easy as well! Buy (new or used) workout clothes that are pleasing to the eye. If you enjoy the pattern, then you will want to wear them. Another way to add to a workout's attractiveness is to buy wireless earbuds. These will give you an excellent excuse to catch up on your favorite show (without feeling guilty about it!).

Now making exercising seem normal is a bit harder. The only way to make it appear normal is if you are doing it already, but that is what you want to change!

Using Dr. Fogg's tiny habit method, and Oettingen and Gollwitzer's implementation intentions can get you there. Your tiny habit could be "After I get home from work, I will workout for five minutes." And the implementation intention could be "If I workout for five minutes, then I will watch 30-minutes of my favorite show."

Before you know it, working out will seem normal, your success will motivate you, and you will gradually increase that amount of time you workout. In time, you will come to see working out as genuinely normal.

Now that you know about tiny habits and the CAN approach it should be reasonably easy for you to succeed! You have all the tools you need, right?

How To Build The Right Habits

Well, first you need to learn to build up the right habits

that will help you crush procrastination. But before you know what the proper habits are, you need to set goals. And, before you make your goals, you need to know how to set the *right* goals.

In the 2010 book *Social Psychological Foundations of Clinical Psychology*, researchers Gabriele Oettingen and Peter M. Gollwitzern tell you how you can do just that. You should frame your intended goals as "I want to achieve Z" [24]. If you want to make achievable goals, you need to make sure they are positive and internally reward based [24]. Positive goals are goals that are framed as "I will..." as opposed to "I will not...". Positively framing your goals motivates you.

Setting negative goals sets up an expectation of withholding something fun. You may even break these "negative" goals to spite yourself. Additionally, basing goals that reward yourself, instead of others, puts less pressure on you. If you set goals that either benefit or reward others, you will feel enormous pressure not to let them down. By focusing on yourself, you can set goals that you know you can achieve on a timeline you know you can meet.

The goals you set should be based on a short time frame and be within your capabilities [24]. Doing this ensures that you have a better chance of reaching them. If you set your goals too far into the future, then they seem more abstract; almost like they are meant for someone else. By placing them on a shorter time frame, there is a greater sense of urgency and immediacy.

Additionally, setting goals that you know you can accomplish ensures that you are not setting yourself up for failure. Think back to the marathon example from the last chapter. If you say: "I will run a marathon within three months", you will have a hard time reaching it. This time frame is short so it seems immediate, but this goal is most likely not capable for you (if it is, then great!).

Setting this goal for yourself when you have a hard-enough time walking up a flight of stairs is not realistic. It is virtually assured that if you try to reach this goal within three months, it will kill you. Instead, try setting a goal like: "I will be able to run a mile within three months." This goal is both on a short time scale and is more aligned with your current capabilities.

Your goals should be challenging while remaining realistic [24]. This way you have a higher chance of meeting, or even exceeding them. Meeting realistic goals will give you a boost of self-confidence that you can carry on with you to your next one.

One of the best ways to make sure your goals are realistic is to use a method called mental contrasting [24]. Mental contrasting, like the name implies, occurs when you imagine a future in which you have obtained your goals, and then think about what is currently standing in your way of achieving them [24].

This process ties your present and future together, so you can analyze whether or not your goals are genuinely realistic [24]. If they are realistic, then you can ascertain what currently is standing in the way of you reaching your goal [24].

Let's return to the running example. "I will run a marathon within three months." Close your eyes and imagine you have accomplished this. You have worked extremely hard for three months and the day has arrived. You feel a sense of pride as you join the other runners. The race begins, and hours later you are crossing the finish line smiling.

Now contrast that with where you currently are. Perhaps you have not run at all since high school. It's been years since then, you've put on some weight, and the only time you run is when you need to catch the elevator. What is stopping you from running a marathon in three months?

Well, lots of things. First of all, time. It takes a lot of time to train for a marathon. If you have not worked out since high school, then the time it takes you to prepare will be even longer. Second, your ability and lack of endurance. Knowing that you get winded going up a flight of stairs, or even running to catch the elevator does not inspire great confidence that you will be able to run for four to five hours straight in three months.

Lastly, you might not be able to go without food for four or five hours at a time. Running a marathon takes *a lot* of energy. Energy that you do not have at the moment. Most likely even if you were able to run that long, you would pass out from exhaustion. Now you realize that this goal you have set for yourself is highly unrealistic.

What about the substitute goal of: "I will be able to run

a mile within three months."? Close your eyes and imagine you have accomplished this goal. You wake up early on a Saturday morning and head on over to the local track. You start running, and it is a breeze. Before you know it, you have completed the mile within ten to fifteen minutes.

What is standing in your way of this goal? Again, there is training time and ability. Working up to running a mile will take some time, but it is indeed doable to get there within three months. You get winded fairly easily right now, but again, it is more likely that you can work up to a mile in three months than it is 26.2 miles.

This indeed is a realistic goal, and you are confident you can reach it. But how will you go about attaining it?

Implementing Your Goals

Once you have set realistic goals, you can then start to

implement them. Implementing your goals is of course challenging. How do you start? Where do you start? What do you do?

You will almost certainly run into some hiccups during the implementation of your goals. There are four main problems that you will probably face: getting started, staying on track, knowing when to stop pursuing not useful goals, and overextending yourself [24]. But what can you do to prevent these problems from occurring? What happens if you don't reach your benchmarks? What if something unexpected happens?

Oettingen and Gollwitzern recommend you implement your goals with a self-regulation technique simplistically named implementation intentions: If X, then Y ; or, if X happens, then I will do Y [24]. Goals are framed as "I want to achieve Z" [24]. The habits that you make to reach those goals are framed as "If X happens, then I will do Y" [24].

This method allows you to plan out what you will do, when and where you will do it, and how you will go about reaching your goals [24]. The "If X happens, then I will Y" formula is similar to Dr. Fogg's tiny habit method so it should be easy for you to perform.

However, instead of tying a new habit to an action you already do using FBM, here you are planning for what will happen in the future. By thinking in depth about what you will do when a particular event comes up, you are freeing yourself of the mental energy of agonizing what to do when that situation occurs [24].

Planning out the habits you will start performing to achieve your goals is a significant first step. Taking time to brainstorm how to achieve your goals will make it easier for you to start going after them. You will gain more significant amounts of energy because you are freed from having to think of a solution to every problem as it occurs. Additionally, you will want to put all of that time you spent brainstorming to good use.

Both the tiny habit method and this if..., then... method use cues to make changing your habits easier by automating them [9] [24]. Here is how you could use implementation intentions to achieve our earlier mentioned goal ("I will be able to run a mile within three months.").

"If I get to work and the elevator is not on the main floor, I will take the stairs to my level." This plan gives a solution (taking the stairs) to the potential future event (elevator not being on the main floor) to help attain the goal (running a mile in three months). What other implementation intentions can you think to help you achieve this goal?

What about the second problem? Are you straying off track? What happens when others try to derail your goals? You can still use this if..., then... method to preplan for those interruptions. When used this way, the process is called suppression-oriented implementation intentions [24].

To get yourself back on track, you can pre-plan for any situations that may arise to cause you to want to give up on your goals. Perhaps you had an awful day at work. You get home, and you don't feel like training to run your mile. Most people would probably crash on the couch and watch tv for the remainder of the night. However, you can prevent yourself from doing this by pre-planning for it.

"If I have a bad day at work, then I will walk around the parking lot before going home." This allows you to get some exercise in while you are still feeling slightly motivated to move. Lots of people find that their energy is zapped after they get home from work. By making a game plan for days like that, you are going to be able to compromise while still working towards your goal (running a mile).

Planning for occasions when your friends (or others) might try and derail you is easier said than done. Or you could make plans with others that would throw off your schedule. But planning for those interactions uses less energy than it takes to confront them without any preparation whatsoever.

A friend you have not seen in a while could invite you out to an early dinner one night. You accept their offer even though you usually make plans to jog after work. Thankfully, you have prepared for this. "If I am unable to jog after work, then I will use the treadmill once I return home." Knowing that you have a plan which takes into account any disruptions is a weight off your shoulders.

You have put all this work into making your habits automatic, making sure you have set the right goals, and have planned for any potential hurdles. But what if the goals you set turn out to not be right for you?

Maybe they are too easy. Perhaps they are too hard. Or, probably since you have been working towards them, you have figured out this goal was not actually what you wanted. What then?

You can still use implementation intentions! Again, you must plan for these situations when you first set your goals and habits. To make this work, you will need to put the adverse situations on the "if" part, and your solution in the "then" part [24]. Your solution will either be to switch to a different method to achieve your goals, or you can change your goal entirely [24].

Back to the running example. Your goal was to run a mile within three months. The deadline is getting closer, and you are nowhere near being able to do that. Thankfully, you prepared for this when you planned out how you would reach your goal. These could be some of the implementation intentions you came up with:

"If I find that I cannot run a mile within three months, then I will re-evaluate my progress and adjust the timeline as needed."

"If I find that I hate running, then I will look into different fitness options (walking/jogging/fitness tapes)."

"If I find that I cannot stand the monotony of running, then I will find a running partner."

You can now look at some of the alternative options you came up with and go with one of them. If none of them appeal to you anymore, you can research alternative options of exercise to do.

The last problem that people run into is overextending themselves. Once again, you can use implementation intentions to prevent overextension from occurring. But since you are using this method, you should find that you are overextending yourself less and less [24]. If you do see yourself doing more than you can handle, fear not! You can still reevaluate your situation via this method.

"If I find that I have overextended myself by ____, then I will evaluate why I did so and take steps to prevent this from happening in the future."

You are now well on your way to beating procrastination because you know the steps to take, and like they say: knowing is half the battle!

How To Embrace A Routine Of Healthy Habits

Now that you know about tiny habits, the CAN approach, how to set and implement goals, and how to counter obstacles it should be reasonably easy for you to succeed! You have all the tools that you need!

But how are you going to embrace these habits? Well, you can utilize operant conditioning. Operant conditioning is a type of learning that transpires through behavior being rewarded or punished [21]. In other words, a person makes a connection between an action they perform and the consequence that they receive [21].

If a positive consequence follows a person's behavior, they will most likely repeat that action; but if a negative consequence follows a person's behavior, they are not likely to perform that behavior again [21]. This is called reinforcement; reinforced behavior will be strengthened in the individual and non-reinforced behavior will be weakened [21].

We can observe three different responses (operants) to behavior: neutral operants, reinforcers, and punishers [21]. Neutral operants do not increase or decrease a behavior; reinforcers increase the likelihood that an action will be repeated, and punishers increase the probability that an act will not be repeated [21].

To help you break your procrastination habits, you could utilize punishments. Punishments can either be used by giving yourself an unpleasant stimulus when you perform the bad behavior, or by taking away an incentive that would be rewarding to you [21].

The unpleasant stimulus you could utilize to stop your bad habits could be as simple as wearing a rubber band around your wrist and snapping it whenever you do that behavior. You do not want to experience pain, so you will try your best to avoid doing those bad behaviors.

Additionally, you could take away something that you enjoy doing. Every time you perform a procrastinatory habit, you can take away time from watching your favorite tv show, time away from games that you like to player playing your favorite game. You could even put a set amount of money, say one dollar in a jar every time you procrastinate. At the end of the week, you would then give that money to a charity.

There are many problems with using punishment to prevent you from performing certain behaviors though. First of all, the response that you are punishing is only suppressed; that is it returns when you stop punishing it [21]. Also, punishment could cause you to react with aggression to your situation [21]. If you did punish yourself with the rubber band, you would not be happy about it and may take out the anger you have at yourself on others.

Lastly, punishments do not help you change your actions to your desired behavior; they reinforce what you should not do [21]. Punishing yourself with the rubber band will lead you to stop that exact type of procrastinatory behavior, but it may unintentionally lead you to pick up other bad behaviors as well.

Positive reinforcement is what you want to give

yourself while you are trying to build habits that will help you break procrastinating. These could be increased tv or game time (or whatever hobby you enjoy doing). But positive reinforcement is not enough; the frequency and schedule of that reinforcement also matter [21].

These are called patterns (or schedules) of reinforcement[21]. Each schedule of reinforcement affects two things. First is the response rate, or the rate that you perform the activity [21]. The second is called the extinction rate, or how soon you give up doing the planned behavior [21].

There are five different patterns of reinforcement, but we will only focus on two: continuous reinforcement, and variable ratio reinforcement [21].

The type of reinforcement that leads to the most extended enforcement of the behavior is variable-ratio reinforcement, and the kind of reinforcement that leads to the shortest enforcement of the action is continuous reinforcement [21].

Continuous reinforcement occurs when you are rewarded for your behavior every time it happens [21]. So, every time you go to the gym, you would get a reward. Every time you sat down to study, you would get a prize. It may seem like a good idea at first, but you will not get far in changing your behavior with this reinforcement.

This continuous reinforcement would lead you to perform the expected behavior at a slow rate, and it would cause you to stop performing the behavior extremely fast [21]. You would become tired of the reward since it occurs every time after you execute the action. Also, you are bribing yourself every time you complete the task. Just knowing that can lead you to stop the right behavior.

Variable-ratio reinforcement, on the other hand, will

allow you to succeed much faster and for a greater length of time. Here, your behavior is rewarded after an unpredictable number of times; think of gambling, fishing, or carnival games [21].

Your response rate would be extremely high here because you do not know when you are being rewarded. Also, you will perform your intended behavior the longest with this method because it is unpredictable. You will receive a rush every time you are rewarded since you were not expecting it.

One way you could randomize the number of times you get rewarded would be to write some big rewards (like going to an amusement park, taking yourself out to a big dinner, etc.) on a handful of slips of paper. Then, you could draw a happy face on a higher number of pieces of paper. You would keep all of these in an opaque container. Every time you finish your new healthy habit; you can shake the jar and pull out a random slip of paper. Doing this will help you keep your new beneficial habits longer.

Chapter 8 Staying Motivated

Be Careful Who You Hang Out With

You have read (most of) this book; you are ready to go out there and make some changes. Nothing can stop you right? Well...

Remember, Dr. Fogg said one of the ways you can make lasting behavior change is to change your environment [9]. Your environment also includes the people you hang out with.

Just think of the adage "If you lie down with dogs, you get up with fleas." You need to be aware of the company you keep because you will pick up their habits.

It's not just an old saying! Drs. Lowe and Haws found that people with the same goals were able to bond together to avoid temptations that would disrupt their progress [19]. However, when people saw that indulging in a behavior would not harm them too much, both felt it was ok to stray from their plan [19]. Who you choose to hang out with will majorly affect your progress. The solution seems to be to hang out with other people who have higher self-control than you.

In 2014, Dzhogleva and Lamberton investigated how people with different self-control habits interacted with each other. They paired together university students and had them work together to solve various tasks [7].

They found that when two students with high self-control were paired together, they did not make many indulgent choices [7]. When two students with low self-control worked together, both decided to indulge [7].

These results were expected; pairing up two students with high self-control would allow them to reinforce each other's efforts to abstain from temptation, whereas two students with low self-control would strengthen each other's tendency to indulge in temptation. If one high and low self-control student were placed together, that should mean the group would be able to resist temptation, right?

Counterintuitively, when a student with high self-control was paired with one with low self-control, that pair tended to indulge in temptation [7]. The explanation for this was the student who had more self-control wanted to "keep the peace," so they willingly allowed their partner's feelings to overshadow theirs [7].

So, is it better to avoid working with a person who has a lower sense of self-control than you? Or for you to avoid working with someone with higher self-control for fear of bringing them down? Not necessarily. If a person with low self-control is externally motivated to better themselves, then they will not "drag down" the partner with higher self-control [7].

This is great news! Since you are reading this book, that means you want to change your behavior. If you are friends with people who have better self-control skills than you, you can ask them for help and feel ok doing it. However, if you have friends who have the same or similar tendencies as you, it probably is a good idea to have a chat with them to see if they can help you out on your journey.

How To Get And Stay Motivated

You should be pumped up and ready to plan out all of your goals, the habits you are going to start changing, and the plans you will make when obstacles occur. You will probably stay motivated (and diligent) in making these changes for a week or two, maybe even a month. But, how are you going to keep your motivation up?

After a while, it will seem like a drag to keep going.

That might be because it takes anywhere from 18 to 254 days to make a new habit stick [18]. That is anywhere from two and a half to just over 36 weeks! How can anyone possibly stay motivated that long?

Maslow's Hierarchy Of Needs

Before we talk about how to stay motivated, first we need to talk about our needs. And what better way to do that than talk about Maslow's Hierarchy of Needs.

There are five different levels of primary or core needs: physiological, safety, love, esteem, and self-actualization [20] which can be formed into the shape of a pyramid. Physiological needs form the foundation of the pyramid, and self-actualization is at the top of the pyramid.

Physiological needs are the base needs a human needs to live and thrive: air, water, food, shelter, sleep, clothing, and sex and reproduction [20]. All of these are pretty self-explanatory. Without satisfying any of these needs, we risk losing our lives. A person who is lacking in all five levels of needs will focus on fulfilling their physiological needs first [20]. It is only when these most basic of needs are satisfied that their attention is returned to the other higher levels [20].

Sustenance is needed to function and think clearly. Trying to accomplish your goals will be nigh impossible if your stomach is growling at you. Lack of sleep will make it extremely hard to focus on anything else. You will be focusing solely on finding adequate shelter so you have a warm place to catch some shut-eye.

After physiological needs are met, safety needs take over. Safety needs will also highly drive an individual, and will sometimes overpower physiological needs if one is desperate enough [20]. Safety needs are the need to feel secure in the environment, having employment, resources, health, property, and insurance [20]. Nowadays, most people are safe in their environment; they do not have to worry about war, epidemics, or natural catastrophes causing damage in their lives [20].

Being secure in your present and in the knowledge that you will be covered in the future (through jobs, insurance, etc.) eases your mind and allows you to level up to love needs.

Love needs cause a person to crave affection, family, intimacy, and an overall sense of connection to people around them [20]. People want to feel like they belong, that they are a part of something bigger than themselves. Humans are social creatures, and without enough social interaction, we will not be able to rise to the next level.

When an individual feels that they are loved enough, they will then start to seek out ways to fulfill their esteem needs. These are the needs to have self-respect, self-esteem, respect from others [20]. Other requirements at this level include independence, freedom, and the desire to be appreciated by others for one's accomplishments [20]. A person wants to show others that they can survive in the world on their own, but at the same time also wants their approval and friendship.

Once all of the previous needs are met, then you can start satisfying your self-actualization needs. Maslow states, "Self-actualization is the desire to become more and more what one is, to become everything that one is capable of becoming" [20]. When you reach the peak of the needs pyramid, you are at the point where you are ready to fulfill your potential. You want to transform yourself into the person that you know you can be.

Unlike the other tiers of the pyramid, self-actualization will vary from person to person [20]. The four lower levels of the pyramid have universal outputs. Everyone needs to satisfy their physiological needs; everyone needs to feel safe; everyone needs love and esteem to be a functional member of society. People may use similar techniques to become the most and the best they can be, but their outcomes will be just as unique as they are.

You most likely have satisfied many levels of your needs. You're satiated, feel secure with your place in society, and have loving family and friends (or at least a reliable social network). However, there is a chance that you lack fulfillment at the esteem level (as most of us do!). And it is likely you have not reached full self-actualization, as few people have [20].

But that is ok! The mere fact that you are here means that you want to change. Your self-esteem and self-respect are high enough that you took the initiative to read this book. You *are* motivated to change because you set out to satiate your need for esteem without even knowing it. You have just learned about some of the many tools you need to increase your self-esteem (and later self-actualization) are in this book; you just need to stay motivated!

Before we get into ways to stay motivated, we need to talk about another theory, this time in regards to motivation: Self-Determination Theory (SDT).

Self-Determination Theory

Self-determination theory tries to understand peoples motivations and personalities through highlighting their penchant to grow and achieve self-actualization by satisfying their basic needs of autonomy, competence, and relatedness [15].

Autonomy refers to a person's ability to make choices based on their free will; competence is the control a person has over their actions, and relatedness is a person's ability to relate and connect to others [15].

Both autonomy and competence correspond to the esteem level of Maslow's hierarchy of needs, and relatedness corresponds to the love level. If these three needs are met, it becomes easy for you to grow as a person and fulfill self-actualization [15].

A persons personality and motivation are partially developed when they internalize the parts of societies goals and norms that match their values [15]. This internalization lets people feel that they are acting on societies goals and standards not because they have to, but because they choose to [15].

In other words, people take the pieces of society that most appeal to them as an individual and make them part of their personality or motivation.

Types Of Internalization

There are four different types of internalization: 1) external regulation, 2) introjection, 3)identification, and, 4) integration [15].

External regulation occurs when rewards and punishments from others control a person's behavior [15]. This could be praise or criticism from a teacher or parent. Or it could be work performance reviews and bonus from your boss.

Introjection happens when a person takes outsiders rewards and punishments and apply them to themselves without fully believing in them [15]. An example would be taking your parents praise and criticisms to heart without fully believing in them.

Identification is the appreciativeness a person has for external regulation [15]. That is, you see the value in others praise and criticisms of you.

Lastly, integration takes place when a person absorbs different forms of external regulation to make them a part of their values and needs [15]. Here, you take the praises and criticisms of yourself and make them a part of who you are. This process allows you to better yourself.

Internalization is not a bad thing. It allows us to be functioning members of society. At times, people stop internalizing and can start to feel negatively pressured, but this lasts for a short time [15]. If people have a good foundation and support system, they should not feel this way for long and spring back to doing what they love.

Causality Orientation

To round out self-determination theory, we have causality orientation. Causality orientation is the measure of the extent that an individual self-regulates [15]. There are three types of causality orientation, autonomy, control, and impersonal [15]

Autonomy orientation determines how inclined a person is to look for experiences that will enhance their self-determination and growth [15]. A person with high autonomy orientation is likely to be highly motivated and will go after things on their own.

Control orientation is how inclined a person is to base their behavior on what outside influences want and expect, as well as how likely they are to feel that their behavior is outside their control [15]. People who have a high control orientation are more likely to wait for others to tell them what to do. They are also expected to be less motivated.

Impersonal orientation is how inclined a person is to dwell on their faults and how likely they are to behave unintentionally [15]. People with high impersonal orientations will have a hard time motivating themselves to do what is needed to be done.

People who have a high level of autonomy orientation

and lower levels of controlled and impersonal orientations will be most likely to reach their full potential [15]. That's not to say that if you feel you have a higher level of controlled and impersonal orientations that you will never reach your potential!

People will naturally reach their full potential when they can fulfill their basic psychological needs (remember, autonomy, competence, relatedness) [15]. If you are struggling at the moment, that's okay! You have not had the opportunity to nurture your authentic self yet. Reading this means that you are ready to start doing that! And that you are truly

You also know what to look for now when you are feeling in a funk. From now on you can make sure your base needs are met. You can identify what is making you motivated and what is tearing you down. After you address all of those things, you will have more motivation (and it will continue to grow every time you do this!).

Finally, we have some practical ways to stay motivated.

Ways To Stay Motivated

Put Up Motivational Sayings!

Take some time to print out motivational quotes and post them around your house. Seeing these every day will remind you that you can do this. You could even print out motivational stories and leave them in places where you will be for a while (in your living room, in the dining room, on your desk, etc.). See if you can find stories from people who have been in your situation before!

Give Yourself Mini-Challenges!

Studying for a test and waiting for the hour to be up? Are you trying to get a certain number of pages done for your report? Challenge yourself! Make a mnemonic to help you remember tough concepts, or better yet a song! Try to get a paragraph written by the time your co-worker comes back in from their break. What other ways can you find to make your work fun?

Break It Down!

Are you facing a massive report at work? An enormous project at school? Break them down into chunks! Take the time to outline what you need to do for each project and do one thing every day! Doing this makes the task seem less massive, and you'll be motivated to do small jobs. Seeing the incremental progress you make will leave you feeling great.

Chart Your Successes!

On a related note, chart your successes! Keep a journal (or keep track on a sheet of paper next to your desk or in a folder), so you have a visual representation of all the work you have done. Use bar graphs to keep track of the number of pages you've written, or the chapters you've read. If you are tracking your weight, create a line graph to see your progress over time. When you see the improvement you have made, it will put a smile on your face.

Work Distraction Free!

Take a look at your working environment. Are you trying to work somewhere that plays loud music or is full of noisy people? Or perhaps you are trying to work at home. Are siblings or cuddly pets getting in your way? Is your phone notifying you of every status update and news story as it comes in?

Then change it! If you need a quiet place to work or study, try the library or community center. Do better with some noise? Plug in your headphones and listen to music, but stay away from people who could potentially distract you. If you work at home, tell your family what your work or study hours are and not to bother you during them (unless it is an emergency!).

Turn off the status and update notifications on your phone, or at least reduce the number that pop up throughout the day. Or, check to see if your phone has a "Do Not Disturb" setting and turn that on when you are trying to work. Some phones even let you set it to "Priority Only" so only the people you select can call you (in case there is an emergency!).

Take Breaks!

Something that a lot of people make the mistake of is trying to *force* motivation to come to you. More often than not, this will occur when you have been working on something for a long time. When you find your motivation (and your attention) starting to wane, it is a good idea to take a quick break. A good rule of thumb is to break for 10-15 minutes after every hour of work you complete.

Find A Buddy!

If you and a friend have similar goals, you can work

together to keep each other motivated. Even if you have different goals, you can still help keep each other on track. Tell each other what your plans are for that day and check in with each other at night. If both of you need more than that, you can check in on each other throughout the day. Or after every strenuous activity you complete. This check-in could be in person, text, phone, email, or video messaging. Whatever way you choose, make it consistent.

Having A Day Off Is Ok!

If you work too hard for too long, you will be at risk for burnout. Once you burn out, you will not feel like doing anything for a very long time. As a result, your work will back up, and you will be even less motivated to return to it.

Taking a day off can help you recover mentally and physically. Giving your brain time to process the information you have learned throughout the week, or your body to heal, will ensure that you will have a ton of motivation to bring to the next week!

Conclusion

We have gone over a lot! Here is a brief overview.

In Chapter 1 we learned that over 20% of American adults are chronic procrastinators. Executive functions are the mental processes that regulate our thoughts, behaviors, actions, concentration, and they allow us to process information.

In Chapter 2, we learned that there are two types of behavior regulation; assessment (people who use this type the most are "thinkers") and locomotion (people who use this type the most are "doers"). Thinkers are more likely to be procrastinators.

In Chapter 3, we learned that procrastinators are more likely to be impulsive, experience intrusive thoughts (daydreams and rumination), and they tend to lack perseverance. Perfectionism can lead to burnout. Burnout occurs when the balance of workload (demands) and social support (resources) are unbalanced. Perfectionistic concerns are more associated with burnout. Being imperfect is ok.

In Chapter 4, we learned that procrastination and impulsiveness effect how you complete your goals. Perfectionism is in your genes. People who have two copies of the normal "COMT" version of the COMT gene are more likely to procrastinate. The serotonin gene SLC6A4 does not affect procrastination.

In Chapter 5, we learned that our brains are always changing. Just getting started on a task creates the right mood because dopamine (the feel-good hormone) is released when we are finished. Procrastination can lead to health problems.

In Chapter 6, we learned about Dr. Fogg and his tiny habits method (After I ____, I will ____). Building up momentum through slow changes and baby steps will build your confidence and cause you to make bigger and more significant changes.

In Chapter 7, we learned that to put our good habits on autopilot we can use the CAN method (make sure our habits are convenient, attractive, and normal). Good practices are those that are framed positively and are on a short time frame. Mental contrasting (thinking of the future you want, and what you are doing now that prevents you from having it) is the best way to see if your goals are reasonable.

To implement our goals, we should use implementation intentions (If____ happens, I will ____). We can embrace our new healthy habits by utilizing positive operant conditioning techniques. We will reward ourselves on a variable-ratio reinforcement schedule. We will give ourselves rewards at unpredictable times to provide us with the greatest chance of sticking with our new habits.

In Chapter 8, we learned that our friends could

influence our decisions. If you want to make positive changes in your life, making friends with people who have higher-self-control will benefit you.

Maslow's Hierarchy of needs consists of five levels, physiological, safety, love, esteem, and self-actualization. Self-determination theory helps us understand how our motivation develops. You will reach your full potential once you can fulfill your base psychological and physiological needs.

Now that you know about these techniques, you can turn your life around! Now go out there and accomplish everything that is on your mind!

References

[1] Bevilacqua, L., & Goldman, D. Genetics of impulsive behavior. *Philos Trans R Soc Lond B Biol Sci, 368*(1615), 20120380. (2013) http://doi.org/10.1098/rstb.2012.0380

[2] Choy, E. E. H., & Cheung, H. Time perspective, control, and affect mediate the relation between regulatory mode and procrastination. *PLoS One, 13*(12), e0207912. (2018) http://doi.org/10.1371/journal.pone.0207912

[3] Collins, A. K., Etienne. Reasoning, Learning, and Creativity: Frontal Lobe Function and Human Decision-Making. *PLoS Biology, 10*(3). (2012) http://doi.org/10.1371/journal.pbio.1001293

[4] Congdon, E. C., Turhan. A Neurogenetic Approach to Impulsivity. *Journal of Personality, 76*(6). (2008) http://doi.org/10.1111/j.1467-6494.2008.00528.x

[5] Di Nocera, F. R., Orlando; Abate, Georgia; Bevilacqua, Arturo. Does the catechol-O-methyltransferase (COMT) Val158Met human

polymorphism influence procrastination? *Organisms. Journal of Biological Sciences, 1*(2), 27-36. (2017) http://doi.org/10.13133/2532-5876_2.7

[6] Diamond, A. Executive Functions. *Annual Review of Psychology, 64,* 135-168. (2013) http://doi.org/10.1146/annurev-psych-113011-143750

[7] Dzhogleva, H., & Lamberton, C. P. Should Birds of a Feather Flock Together? Understanding Self-Control Decisions in Dyads. *Journal of Consumer Research, 41*(2), 361-380. (2014) http://doi.org/10.1086/676599

[8] Fogg, B. J. Fogg's Behavior Model. (2007) http://www-personal.umich.edu/~mrother/KATA_Files/FBM.pdf

[9] Fogg, B. J. (2013). Fogg Method: 3 steps to changing behavior. 2019, from http://www.foggmethod.com/

[10] Friedman, N. P. M., Akira; Young, Susan E.;

DeFries, John C.; Corley, Robin P.; Hewitt, John K. Individual Differences in Executive Functions Are Almost Entirely Genetic in Origin. *Journal of Experimental Psychology, 137*(2), 201-225. (2008) http://doi.org/10.1037/0096-3445.137.2.201

[11] Gustavson, D. E. M., Akira; Hewitt, John K.; Friedman, Naomi P. Genetic Relations Among Procrastination, Impulsivity, and Goal-Management Ability: Implications for the Evolutionary Origin of Procrastination. *Psychological Science, 25*(6), 1178-1188. (2014) http://doi.org/10.1177/0956797614526260

[12] Herd, S. M., Brian; O'Reilly, Randall. (2010). *Dopamine and self-directed learning* Paper presented at the Biologically Inspired Cognitive Architectures, Washington, DC, USA. http://doi.org/10.3233/978-1-60750-661-4-58

[13] Hill, A. P., & Curran, T. Multidimensional Perfectionism and Burnout: A Meta-Analysis. *Pers Soc Psychol Rev, 20*(3), 269-288. (2016) http://doi.org/10.1177/1088868315596286

[14] Kolb, B. Brain and behavioral plasticity in the developing brain: Neuroscience and public policy. *Paediatric & Child Health, 14*(10), 651-652. (2009) http://doi.org/10.1093/pch/14.10.651

[15] Koole, S. L., Schlinkert, Caroline, Maldei, Tobias, Baumann, Nicola. Becoming who you are: An integrative review of self-determination theory and personality systems interactions theory. *Journal of Personality, 87*(1), 15-36. (2019) http://doi.org/10.1111/jopy.12380

[16] Kruglanski, A. W. P., Antonio; Higgins, E. Tory. Experience of Time by People on the Go: A Theory of the Locomotion-Temporality Interface. *Personality and Social Psychology Review, 20*(2), 100-117. (2016) http://doi.org/10.1177/1088868315581120

[17] Kruglanski, A. W. T., Erik P.; Higgins, E. Tory; Atash, M. Nadir; Pierro Antonio; Shah, James Y., Spiegel, Scott. To "Do the Right Thing" or to "Just Do It": Locomotion and Assessment as Distinct self-Regulatory Imperatives.

Personality and Social Psychology, 79(5), 793-815. (2000) http://doi.org/10.1037//0022-3514.79.5.793

[18] Lally, P., van Jaarsveld, C. H. M., Potts, H. W. W., & Wardle, J. How are habits formed: Modelling habit formation in the real world. *European Journal of Social Psychology, 40*(6), 998-1009. (2010) http://doi.org/10.1002/ejsp.674

[19] Lowe, M. L., & Haws, K. L. (Im)moral Support: The Social Outcomes of Parallel Self-Control Decisions. *Journal of Consumer Research, 41*(2), 489-505. (2014) http://doi.org/10.1086/676688

[20] Maslow, A. H. A Theory of Human Motivation. *Psychological Review, 50*(4), 370-396. (1943) http://doi.org/10.1037/h0054346

[21] McLeod, S. A. (2018, 21 Jan 2018). Skinner-Operant Conditioning. 2019, from https://www.simplypsychology.org/operant-conditioning.html

[22] Miyake, A. F., Naomi P. The Nature and

Organization of Individual Differences in Executive Functions: Four General Conclusions. *Current Directions in Psychological Science, 21*(1), 8-14. (2012) http://doi.org/10.1177/0963721411429458

[23] Miyake, A. F., Naomi P.; Emerson, Michael J.; Witzki, Alexander H.; Howerter, Amy. The Unity and Diversity of Executive Functions and Their Contributions to Complex "Frontal Lobe" Tasks: A Latent Variable Analysis. *Cognitive Psychology, 41,* 49-100. (2000) http://doi.org/10.1006/cogp.1999.0734

[24] Oettingen, G. G., Peter M. (2010). Strategies of Setting and Implementing Goals; Mental Contrasting and Implementation Intentions. In J. E. Maddux (Ed.), *Social psychological foundations of clinical psychology* (pp. 114-135). New York.

[25] Procrastinate | Definition of Procrastinate by Merriam-Webster. (2019, 10 Mar). from https://www.merriam-webster.com/dictionary/procrastinate

[26] Procrastination. (2019, 2019). from https://www.psychologytoday.com/us/basics/procrastination

[27] Rebetez, M. M. L., Rochat, L., Barsics, C., & Van der Linden, M. Procrastination as a Self-Regulation Failure: The Role of Impulsivity and Intrusive Thoughts. *Psychol Rep, 121*(1), 26-41. (2018) http://doi.org/10.1177/0033294117720695

[28] Sirois, F. M. Is procrastination a vulnerability factor for hypertension and cardiovascular disease? Testing an extension of the procrastination-health model. *J Behav Med, 38*(3), 578-589. (2015) http://doi.org/10.1007/s10865-015-9629-2

[29] Stoeber, J. O., Kathleen. Positive Conceptions of Perfectionism: Approaches, Evidence, Challenges. *Personality and Social Psychology Review, 10*(4), 295-319. (2006) http://doi.org/10.1207/s15327957pspr1004_2

[30] Tibbett, T. P., & Ferrari, J. R. Return to the origin:

what creates a procrastination identity? *Current Issues in Personality Psychology, 7*(1), 1-7. (2019) http://doi.org/10.5114/cipp.2018.75648

[31] Wansink, B. Change Their Choice! Changing Behavior Using the *CAN* Approach and Activism Research. *Psychology & Marketing, 32*(5), 486-500. (2015) http://doi.org/10.1002/mar.20794

[32] Wu, H., Gui, D., Lin, W., Gu, R., Zhu, X., & Liu, X. The procrastinators want it now: Behavioral and event-related potential evidence of the procrastination of intertemporal choices. *Brain Cogn, 107,* 16-23. (2016) http://doi.org/10.1016/j.bandc.2016.06.005

Disclaimer

The information contained in **"Conquering Procrastination"** and its components, is meant to serve as a comprehensive collection of strategies that the author of this book has done research about. Summaries, strategies, tips and tricks are only recommendations by the author, and reading this book will not guarantee that one's results will exactly mirror the author's results.

The author of this book has made all reasonable efforts to provide current and accurate information for the readers of this book. The author and its associates will not be held liable for any unintentional errors or omissions that may be found.

The material in the book may include information by third-parties. Third-party materials comprise of opinions expressed by their owners. As such, the author of this book does not assume responsibility or liability for any third-party material or opinions.

written expressed and signed permission from the author.